How To Use Machine To Sew Anything

Step by Step Guide on How to Start Using Sewing Machines to Sew and Mend Anything You Want

(Including Sample Projects to Get You Started)

Introduction

Have you been looking to start sewing your own items, or have you been hand-sewing for a while and are looking to make more elegant designs much faster with perfect stitches?

Are you tired of putting in countless hours trying to manually mimic the reliability of a sewing machine in tension and spacing, and would you like to create items in the least time possible and have them turn out to be gorgeously designed?

If this sounds like you, well, you'll be pleased to know that you are in the right place!

This is the book for you, and I'll teach you all you need to know to start using a sewing machine even if you've never touched one before.

I also have a couple of projects lined up to get you started. So, are you ready to get started?

Let's go!

Table of Contents

Chapter 1: What You Need to Know About A Sewing Machine

When you want to create your own clothing, décor, or accessories from scratch within a reasonable time frame, you'll need to get your own sewing machine. Compared to sewing by hand, using a machine is way quicker, and you can create more consistent, stronger stitches.

However, if you don't know what to look for, you might end up with a gadget that will drain your funds rather than serve as an investment. That is why we will be discussing below how to select the ideal sewing machine for beginners.

What Should You Look for When Purchasing a Sewing Machine?

Completing a sewing project by yourself is a great achievement. However, you will require the correct machine for the job to attain this achievement. There is a wide range of sewing machines available with different features. Still, the best for beginners should be durable and simple to use while yielding exceptional stitch quality.

Before you go on the lookout for a sewing machine, you will first have to consider the most essential features and the types of projects you'll be using your machine for.

Here is what you want to look for:

Stitch Number: when starting to learn how to sew, you only require 2 stitches: the zigzag and straight. However, as you advance in the skill, you'll also require additional stitch selections and decorative stitches, so make sure your machine can offer them.

Weight: if you intend to carry the sewing machine to sewing groups or classes, ensure that you go for a portable variety. Select a sewing machine that is light in weight, featuring a handle to make it easier to haul the device around.

Ease Of Use: when it comes to choosing your very first sewing machine, keep in mind, the simpler the machine is, the better. Of course, the machine you select should still feature a sturdy metal frame and basic tools. However, steer clear of devices with features you will not be using. Such machines will only get in your way and make it even more difficult for you to master the machine.

And how will you know the features that will not be of use to you?

Below we have a list of the basic parts of a sewing machine:

Basic Parts of A Sewing Machine

The basic parts of a sewing machine include:

1. Foot Controller

This part of a sewing machine is named logically according to its function, so it is very easy to remember. It is located by the floor below the table where the device is positioned and is operated by pressing your foot on it.

The foot controller regulates the stitching speed – the more pressure you apply on it, the faster your needle will go.

2. Presser Foot

This is the metal plate that keeps your fabric in place by pressing against it and aids in constancy as well. A lever allows you to operate the presser foot by lifting it up and down.

Presser feet are available in different varieties based on the type of sewing you'll be doing. For instance, we have a satin foot for delicate fabrics or a special zipper foot that we use to install zippers

3. Feed Dogs

This is the part with small teeth made of rubber or metal where you will be feeding your fabric to pass under the needle. It helps regulate the stitch length according to how slow or fast the feed dogs move the fabric.

As much as it is possible to use your hands to guide the fabric, don't try pushing it through faster or slowing it down; this is what the feed dogs are for, and if you try doing it yourself, it can result in the needle snapping.

4. Needle

This is perhaps the most obvious part of a sewing machine. It's the slim metallic pole with a hole near where you'll be threading the cotton through and comes to a pointed tip on the other end.

In sewing machines, the needles are screwed in place, and they are available in different sizes.

5. Needle Clamp

This part holds the needle and keeps it from disengaging when the sewing machine is in use.

6. Throat Plate

The throat plate is also called the needle plate. It is a big metallic plate that lies below the presser foot and the needle. It keeps your fabric from being pulled into the machine.

You can remove it to get to the bobbin. The needle plate usually includes markings on it that act as a guide for seam allowances.

7. Arm

This is the part that holds the mechanism for working the needle. It gets its name from how it resembles a curving arm.

8. Bed

This can be described as the whole flat surface of a sewing machine where you'll be resting your fabric. The bed anchors the sewing machine to guarantee stability and offers you a fairly sized working surface as well.

9. Bobbin

A bobbin can simply be described as a spool that is winded with thread around it. It acts as the bottom of the stitching mechanism.

The stitch is made when the needle thread and bobbin thread loop together. The bobbins can either be side or top loading and are usually fixed below the bed (resting place of fabric).

10.   Bobbin Winder

It's a small rod that is usually found on the top right corner of a sewing machine. When you insert an empty bobbin on this fixture, it winds the thread around it with the right tension to produce a bobbin that has been wound evenly.

11. Bobbin Winder Tension Disk

This part is mostly found on the upper central section of a sewing machine. It leads the thread between the spool and the bobbin winder.

12. Bobbin Case

This is the round metallic casing that houses the bobbin. The function of this part is to provide tension to the lower thread.

Ensure that you don't switch bobbin cases between different devices as they are designed in a precise size and shape to fit that particular sewing machine.

13. Spool Holder

It is also called a spool pin. The spool holder is a small rod across which you slide on the main spool to ensure that the spool doesn't come off as you stitch. This part is either fitted at a vertical or horizontal angle. However, the latter is typically better as its feed is smoother.

14. Side Plate

This part is metallic and encloses the bobbin case. You can easily remove it to replace the bobbin.

15. Balance Wheel

It is also called the handwheel or flywheel. The balance wheel makes it possible for you to operate the needle manually.

You can turn the handwheel to lower or raise the needle, mostly to modify the needle's sewing height. This part is usually located on the side of a sewing machine at the right end.

16. Stitch Selector

As its name suggests, the stitch selector is used for choosing the stitch you would like to use, such as a straight stitch or zigzag stitch. Current sewing machines have buttons for this task while the older ones have a dial for selecting the stitch.

17. Reverse Lever

It's also called a backstitch button. It is a lever we use to reverse the stitching direction immediately.

We mostly use the backstitch button at the start and finish of stitching to tighten the fabric's thread firmly in place.

18. Tension Regulator

This part is responsible for regulating the tension of the machine's top thread. To make sure that you achieve neat stitches, you'll want to balance the tension of the top thread and the bobbin thread.

If your tension is too taut, the stitches will collect tightly and wrinkle your fabric. Then again, if the tension is loose, your stitches will unfasten. Modify your tension by altering the digital settings (new machines) or flipping the dial (older machines).

19. Take Up Lever

The take up lever may be positioned on the front side of a sewing machine or it can be concealed from the inside view. The upper thread passes through this lever.

This part moves simultaneously up and down with the needle. Every time you feed your fabric underneath the needle, make sure to adjust the take up lever to prevent your fabric from getting caught and torn.

Chapter 2: Classifications of Sewing Machines

Sewing machines are basically classified according to their functions, but we can also classify them based on their features, such as embroidery, quilting, or sewing.

There are 5 categories of sewing machines, which I have classified according to features.

These are:

1. Mechanical or domestic sewing machines

2. Automated or computerized sewing machines

3. Electronic sewing machines

4. Serger or Overlock sewing machines

5. Embroidery machines

Let's look at the machines in depth.

1. Mechanical Sewing Machines

Mechanical sewing machines are also known as treadle sewing machines, tailoring machines, or manual machines. With these machines, the user performs the basic settings manually.

We can classify manual sewing machines into 2:

- *Old model treadle* (where you operate the lever with your foot)

- *Hand-based* (where you use your hands)

Both classifications operate on human effort, although electric motors are now replacing those efforts.

The model and the manufacturing company determine the body type of a mechanical sewing machine. The body is usually made of aluminum and is usually black in color. These old model sewing machines can either be table-based or stand-based.

Since they don't require the user to be experienced in sewing, manual sewing machines are simple to handle. This is the perfect machine if you want to learn sewing from basics or are interested in taking up tailoring at home for household items.

Features

A domestic sewing machine features an adjustable stitch length, adjustable tension, bottom loading bobbin, inbuilt presser feet, and single (reverse and straight) stitch.

Some of the most recent manual sewing machines include one or two advanced features, such as a small LED screen for selecting the stitch pattern.

Advantages of Mechanical Machines

- Mechanical sewing machines are cheap.

- Easy to repair.

- They come with very limited features that are simple to understand.

- Effective in simple stitching.

Disadvantages of Mechanical Sewing Machines

- Not ideal for sewing thicker fabrics such as leather and denim.

- You have to keep threading the needle over and over, which can be very annoying.

- They have just one inbuilt straightforward stitching mechanism.

- The treadle devices are not easily movable, and they take up more space.

- You can't use it for other decorative crafting functions such as embroidery.

2. Computerized Sewing Machines

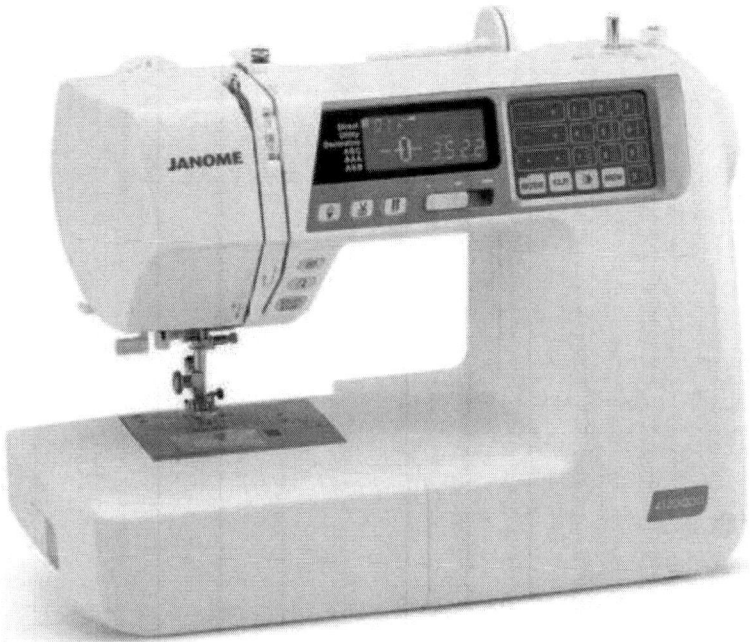

These are state-of-the-art sewing machines that you can connect to design loaded cards, computers, or the internet. Computerized sewing machines are huge, heavy-duty, and they work very fast. They are mostly ideal for industrial functions where you can design large-scale fabrics within a short amount of time.

Features

Automated sewing machines feature several needles and spool spinners for thread spools of different colors for sewing, smocking, quilting, embroidery, and other crafts.

The inbuilt stitch capacity for these machines is at least 50 but not more than 200. These sewing machines also include a special feature known as Autopilot Stitching Mode, where the device can control the stitch strength, thread tension, and speed (the stitches produced in a minute).

Advantages

- They are heavy-duty and can handle any type of fabric.

- You can download and design or pattern from the internet.

- Impressive stitch capacity.

Disadvantages

- They are costly. The prices differ based on the features available on a particular model.

- You need to watch a tutorial or read the manual to know how to use other features. The manufactures typically provide a manual.

- Difficult to correct technical problems such as data loading, errors, and connectivity issues.

3. Electronic Sewing Machine

An Electronic sewing machine can simply be described as a combination of computerized and mechanical sewing machines. Some use battery and others use electricity according to the model – the heavy-duty models typically operate on electricity.

If you are big on DIYs, you'll be pleased to know that these devices are very handy in DIY decorative crafting. If you find these additional features unnecessary or don't sew regularly, it's better to invest in a manual sewing machine.

Features

These sewing machines have quite a lot to offer. They are for professional sewing. Electronic sewing machines are compact-sized, motorized, and free-arm, with some models featuring an LCD screen for selecting the patterns accordingly.

These devices feature an inbuilt needle threader, automatic thread cutter, adjustable presser foot, twin needle compatibility, auto tripling bobbin, and loading drop in bobbin. They also feature adjustable needle positioning, adjustable stitch width and length, reverse stitch lever, inbuilt stitch capacity of at least 7 stitches, and an add-on option for more features.

They have good quality stitching and are great for hemming, embroidering, hemming zip fixing, smocking, buttonholes stitch, blind stitch, and quilting.

Advantages

- They are lightweight, which makes them portable.

- Good for tailors and professionals.

Disadvantages

- Requires training to use.

- Requires a professional to repair.

- Expensive to purchase and maintain compared to mechanical sewing machines.

4. Embroidery Sewing Machines

The purpose of these machines is to design various embroidery patterns on your fabric. You can attach an embroidering presser foot to an electronic sewing machine to use it for embroidery.

If you'd like to learn basic embroidery, it is recommended to select a zigzag machine as a beginner. For skilled level or professionals, it's better to go for an electronic sewing machine model with the embroidering feature and various patterns.

Most variations of computerized embroidering machines are produced for industrial functions.

Advantages

- Best for tailors/professionals.

Disadvantages

- Costly to purchase and maintain compared to manual sewing machines.

5. Serger or Overlocker Sewing Machine

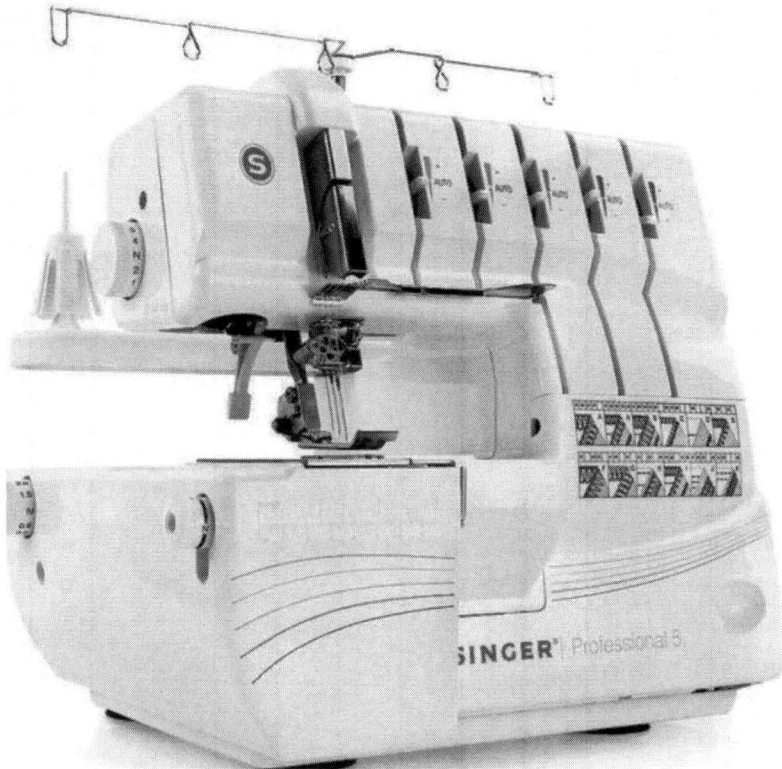

Serger sewing machines are useful for overlocking or seaming the fabric – they are used to sew or join the edges of fabric together. Professionals typically use these machines to give their garments a finishing touch.

The serger is also used by garment industries to edge napkins, elastic hemming or seaming in edging curtains, overlocking on pillow covers, lingerie designing, and other decorative crafting. You can choose to modify the length and width of your stitches.

The capacity of your thread stitch determines the price of the overlocker sewing machine. Patterns of overlock stitches are based on the number of threads it utilizes:

- Single-threaded overlock stitch

- 2 threaded overlock stitch

- 3-thread overlock stitch

- 4 threaded overlock stitch

- 5 threaded overlock stitch

The weakest loop is a single-threaded overlock stitch; the more the number of threads you use to edge your loop, the stronger it becomes. Also, single-threaded overlockers as cheaper than other 5 or 4 threaded stitch overlockers.

Features

This sewing machine features an inbuilt cutter, which is a blade that trims the unequal edges of your fabric while at the same time edging the textile or garment.

The device typically creates stitch loops over your fabric edge.

Advantages

- Possible to alter the length and width of your stitches.

Disadvantages

- More expensive compared to domestic sewing machines.

Next up, we'll look at the best sewing machines for beginners.

Chapter 3: Best Sewing Machines for Beginners

As we had mentioned earlier, there are a wide range of sewing machines available out there, and if you are not careful enough, you might end up taking a machine that will be problematic to use or costly to maintain, especially since you don't have much experience with them. Below I have listed the ideal examples of sewing machines that any beginner can use with ease:

Best First Sewing Machine

Start 1304 Sewing Machine for Beginners

Start 1304 is an impressive machine with controls that are simple to follow and an accessible backstitch. It features multiple needles, bobbins, and presser feet.

This machine weighs only 7 pounds, making it excellent for small spaces and is easily portable. This model is very popular on Amazon with sparkling reviews and you can buy it there for $115.20.

Best Serger for Beginners

Juki MO654DE Serger

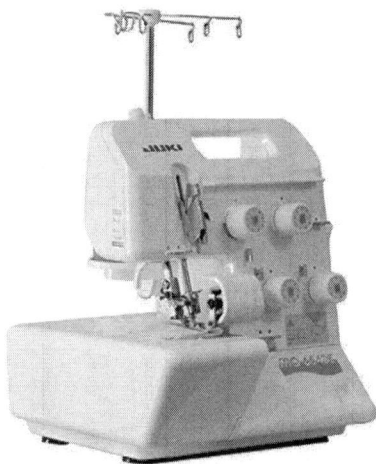

This particular sewing machine cuts your fabric to a clean edge and keeps the raw edge from fraying by wrapping threads around it – something that other sewing machines cannot do. A serger gives the final seam a neat, professional appearance.

The Juki MO654DE is the most suitable serger for beginners featuring basics such as automatic rolled hem mechanism and 2,3,4 thread options to finish the edges cleanly.

Additionally, this machine features a high speed of 1,500 stitches in a mere minute – this will come in handy as you get more advanced. The Juki serger is popular among the sewing community for being powerful while at the same time not so noisy.

You can get it for $369.68 from Amazon.

Best Heavy-Duty Machine for Beginners

Singer 4452 Heavy Duty Sewing Machine

This classic model is a popularly known machine for sewing heavy-duty fabrics such as leather and denim. This machine has a robust motor that can yield 1,100 stitches in a minute, making it easy to speed through your projects in a short amount of time.

The motor is also strong enough to work thick seams effortlessly. Singer heavy duty provides a variety of multiple buttonhole options and 32 different stitches without seeming too overwhelming.

For your own convenience, it is recommended that you only use plastic bobbins when handling this machine. You can purchase this model online on Amazon for $200.12.

Best Embroidery Sewing Machine for Beginners

Brother SE625 Computerized Sewing and Embroidery Machine

Sewing machines that feature embroidery mechanisms are usually costly and are very advanced, with Brother SE625 being the most common and affordable.

With this model, you get a 4 by 4 embroidery field where you can see each of your designs fully colored on the LCD screen, making it easy for you to make modifications such as switching the thread color. (Note: the embroidery field includes a loop, embroidery foot, and arm.)

Brother SE625 includes multiple features that make it very easy to use, such as a drop-in bobbin for avoiding jams, free arm, LED-lit work area, and an automatic needle threader. When you remove the embroidery arm, this machine remains a fully functional sewing machine.

The device also comes with 80 embroidery designs, 103 stitches, and a USB port you can use for uploading your own designs or you can get a wide range of designs by browsing Brother online.

You can get this model on Amazon for $550.10

Best Sewing Machine for Beginners Overall

7363 Confidence Sewing Machine

If you are a beginner with the desire to engage in more advanced projects in the future, this is the sewing machine for you. This model features a drop in bobbin for easier threading instead of the standard style bobbin.

What makes this machine even more ideal for beginners is having an adjustable speed where you are able to go at your own pace when learning to sew with it. In addition, the device includes a stop/start setting that makes it possible to quickly stop if you slip up.

7363 Confidence sewing machine has a programmable needle up/down, an inbuilt needle threader, 6 buttonhole options, and 100 stitches – qualities that make it good for sewing anything you like!

As if the features we've mentioned are not impressive enough, this model is able to adjust the tension automatically according to different fabrics.

You can get this sewing machine at joann.com for $189.99.

Sewing Machine That Offers The Best Value for Beginners

Cs141wpu Portable Mini Sewing Machine

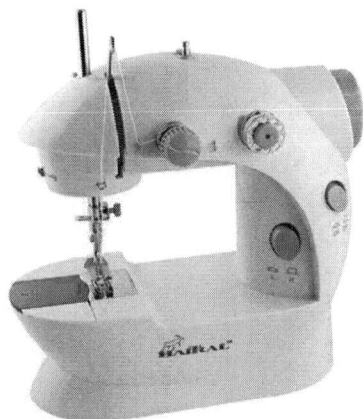

This portable mini sewing machine is the simplest and modernized of all sewing machines, and it only costs 20 dollars. It is a fully functional sewing machine that is very easy to carry as it weighs below 3 pounds. This model has only one stitch, making it excellent for simple small projects. It features an inbuilt lamp, a removable extension table, and a side thread cutter.

Note: Since Cs141wpu Portable Mini Sewing Machine does not include a backstitch, you'll have to sew over your ends once more to secure the stitches.

Now that you've picked your sewing machine, let's look at the types of fabrics out there.

Chapter 4: All About The Fabrics

The question that you might now be thinking is, *what makes fabric easy to work with?*

When you start learning how to sew using a machine, it is best to work with simple fabrics.

Below are the characteristics of easy-to-sew fabrics:

1. Not Too Thick Or Thin

With thin fabrics, it is common to stretch them out as they are easily overhandled. As for thick fabrics, they require more precision when stitching since it is more likely to skip stitches.

It is also problematic to maneuver the thick fabric pattern pieces underneath the needle and presser foot. So, find a nice regular-sized fabric in your preferred color.

2. Minimal or No Stretching

When sewing, it is very easy to overstretch fabrics that are stretchable. It will take some time to develop a natural impulse for handling stretchable fabric while you sew – recognizing when to pull and when to leave the feed dogs and foot to their work.

To make matters worse, if you mess up a seam, the chances of damaging (misshaping, to be specific) the fabric as you undo your stitches is very high.

3. No Need for Special Presser Feet

As a beginner, I advise you to steer clear of fabrics with suggestions (walking, non-stick) requiring the use of a special presser foot as it may turn out to be difficult to work with, or it will be too difficult for an all-purpose foot at least.

Before deciding to purchase such fabric, ask yourself whether it will be worth it to switch between presser feet or buy a different presser foot.

Fabrics Beginners Should Avoid

As a beginner, you should steer clear of the following fabrics:

1. Exceptionally Thick Fabric

As we had mentioned earlier, thick fabrics are hard to move evenly underneath the needle, resulting in uneven stitches. Thick fabrics also require tension adjustments and heavy-duty needles – things you should not concern yourself with on a beginner level.

2. Slippery Fabrics

Cutting fabric that is slippery accurately is a tricky and slow process. Not to mention the extra basting and pining and taking care to keep your fabric from slipping off the sewing table.

3. Exceptionally Thin Fabric

Similar to thick fabric, thin fabric also requires making tension adjustments and using particular needles to yield even stitches. Also, when pressing thin fabric, it is easy to warp your pattern pieces.

Moreover, it can be very irritating how thin fabric gets caught on the throat plate's needle opening.

4. Embellished Fabric

This type of fabric is very appealing. However, it demands a tiresome form of special treatment where you have to take out every sequin along the seam allowances before stitching the seams.

Failure to do that could cause your needle to break or shatter the sequins, and the pieces may get trapped in the machine.

Types Of Fabrics and Their Examples

As you might be well aware, there are many fabrics available. Most patterns have a fabric recommendation, so, below I have listed the various classifications of fabrics and their examples to guide you when shopping for fabrics.

They include:

Types of fabrics	Examples of the fabric
Lightweight fabrics	Muslin, georgette, Crepe de chine, Silk chiffon, Organdie, Voile, Cotton lawn, Thai silk, Cotton batiste, Silk habotai, Silk organza
Openwork Fabrics or Mesh Fabrics	Tarlatan, Cape net, Lace, Borderie Anglaise, Eyelet fabric, Buckram, net fabrics (illusion mesh knits), Assuit, Bobbinet, Tulle
Medium-weight fabrics	Cashmere, Crepe de China, Gingham, Raw silk, Cheesecloth, Gabardine, Flannel, Sateen, Chintz, Damask, Gauze, Poplin
Plied fabrics	Brushed denim, Felt, Flannelette, Microfiber, Ultra suede, Suede, Milt

	soft pile – flannel, Boucle (loops), Terrycloth, Velveteen, Velour, Plush, Astrakhan, Chenille, Velvet, Faux fur, Fur
Heavyweight fabrics	Chenille, Upholstery fabric, Towelling fabric, Tweed, Tartan, Fleece, Denim, Canvas
Shiny glossy fabrics	Cire, Polished cotton, Sateen, Silk (and all its variations), Satin
Ribbed Fabric	Calvary twill, Chino, Bedford cord, Pique, Faille Taffeta, Poplin (Broadcloth), Serge, Drill, Whipcord, Moire, Bengaline, Grosgrain, Corduroy, Gabardine, Denim

The Best Fabrics for Beginners to Practice How to Sew

If you are a beginner, go ahead and stock up on the following fabric:

1. Cotton

Cotton is perhaps the most forgiving and simplest to use fabric. It is versatile with different options for weight making it great for multilayered crafts, from simple designs to more detailed projects.

Cotton is comfortable to wear and easy to maintain in addition to being cheap. Consider beginning with easy patterns such as pillow covers, blankets, bags, pants, skirts, or shirts. Before you begin sewing, make sure to prewash your cotton fabric as it typically shrinks.

2. Muslin

This is a form of cotton fabric that is extremely simple to work with. It is very versatile (where you can use it for coarse and delicate clothing) and has a plain weave.

This fabric is commonly used in making blouses, washcloths, upholstery, blankets, quilts, dresses, and other forms of clothing. Muslin is reasonably priced enough that some experienced sewers use it for practice before they move on to cut the more high-priced fabrics for the final design.

3. Polyester

This fabric is very popular for beginners. It is a woven synthetic fabric that is crease-resistant and typically lightweight. Polyester is moisture resistant and is excellent for home furnishings and apparel.

You can use this fabric to make items like upholstered furniture, blankets, bedsheets, jackets, pants, shirts, and hats. Polyester is an economical substitute for natural fabrics and a perfect fabric for practicing sewing.

Suitability of the Fabric to Particular Garments

The best fabrics for different garments are indicated below;

1. Best Fabric To Sew Pants

Go for fabrics that aren't too rigid or hard, or you will not feel comfortable wearing them. Flannel, denim, and linen are great choices. Select wool (both wood blends and 100%) for colder climates.

The type of pants (whether jeans, unstructured pants, tailored trousers, or combined) basically determine the fabric to use. You can also make some very comfortable pants using Corduroy.

2. Best Fabrics to Sew Kid's Clothing And Stuff

For kids, it is recommended to use all cotton fabrics. You can select cotton lawn, cotton satin, cotton twill, or cotton satin stretch. You may also use knit fabrics such as wool knits. Steer clear of synthetic textiles.

3. Best Fabrics to Sew Skirts

Cotton lawn with beautiful prints, Ponte Roma knit, silk jersey, and lightweight cotton are all great for sewing skirts. You may also purchase silk that is printed and rayon in charmeuse, georgette, chiffon, and crepe.

Fine knits in silk, microfiber, and rayon are also suitable. Other ideal fabrics for sewing skirts include stretch velvet, lycra blends, soft wool, and drapey rayons.

4. Best Fabrics to Sew Jackets

Flannel, linen, or wool, particularly wool tweeds and wool crepe, are all great for making jackets. You can also make a nice, free-flowing jacket using lightweight velvet knits.

5. Best Fabrics to Sew Dresses

For making dresses, organza, silk chiffon, lace, velvet, taffeta, satin, and raw silk work great. However, the type of dress also determines the fabric to use.

For instance, medium-weight fabrics, including some elastane (spandex) are good for a fitting body rip-off dress. If you want to make drapey dresses, go for lightweight fabrics such as charmeuse, challis, crepe, and jersey.

6. Best Fabrics to Sew a Lining Inside Your Garments

The most commonly used fabrics for sewing a lining are cotton and rayon acetate.

7. Best Fabric To Sew Shirts/ Blouses

To make shirts or blouses it is recommended to buy Linen, batiste, lightweight woven broadcloth, eyelet, poplin, seersucker, faille, twill, chintz, cambric, chiffon, and lightweight cotton fabric. To make airy tops, silky satin fabric is perfect for the job.

Buying the Fabric

Before you go shopping for the fabric, you should have a sewing pattern in mind of what you intend to make. Once you have the pattern, you will have a better idea of how much fabric to purchase and the types of fabric you are looking for. You could buy any buttons, zips, or threads as well to match your design.

It may, however, not turn out that way. You may come across some exceptional fabric that you simply can't just pass up. If this happens, obtain 3m of that fabric to have a variety for when you are ready to sew.

When you go shopping for fabric:

- Confirm that the fabric you choose is among the recommended ones for the sewing pattern you select.

- Roll out the fabric bolt a bit and check how the fabric flows. Feel it to ensure that it fits with the pattern you want to make.

- Check the label for care instructions and fiber content. If the fabric is too demanding to maintain, just find another one.

- Picture your intended design created in the fabric you select. How does it look? Does the fabric color suit you?

- Check the fabric width. Fabrics come in various widths: mostly 45" (115 cm) and 60" (150 cm). Determine the length of fabric you will require by looking at your sewing pattern. Ensure that you purchase enough fabric for a 10% shrinkage on washing to be on the safe side.

- Take your time. Take as much time as you can to make sure that you like how the fabric you have selected looks, you like how it feels under your touch, and you have it in the correct size.

Where to Buy Your Fabric Online

- Joann.com

- Minted.com

- Michaels.com

- Dickblick.com

- Westelm.com

- Calicocorners.com

- Moodfabrics.com

- Loomdecor.com

- Spoonflower.com

How exactly do you use a sewing machine with the fabrics in mind?

Chapter 5: How to Use a Sewing Machine

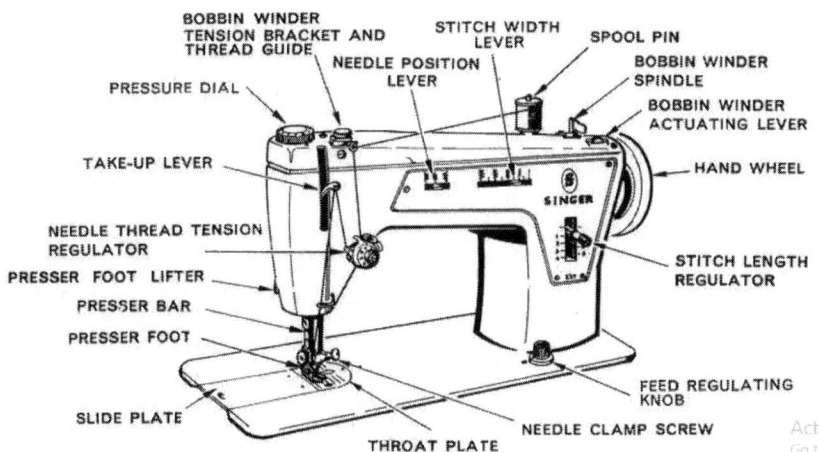

BOBBIN WINDER
TENSION BRACKET AND   STITCH WIDTH
THREAD GUIDE   LEVER   SPOOL PIN
                    NEEDLE POSITION   BOBBIN WINDER
PRESSURE DIAL   LEVER   SPINDLE
                                                  BOBBIN WINDER
                                                  ACTUATING LEVER

TAKE-UP LEVER   HAND WHEEL

                                                    SINGER

NEEDLE THREAD TENSION
REGULATOR
PRESSER FOOT LIFTER   STITCH LENGTH
                                                   REGULATOR
PRESSER BAR
PRESSER FOOT

                                               FEED REGULATING
                                               KNOB
SLIDE PLATE
                              NEEDLE CLAMP SCREW
        THROAT PLATE

Before anything else, you need first to set up your machine.

Setting Up Your Sewing Machine

Step 1: Position The Machine On A Counter, Desk, Or Sturdy Table

Find a chair of a comfortable height as the table you select. Set up your machine to have the machine's body on the right side and the needle end on your left side.

However, don't plug in the machine yet as you first need to check some things and familiarize yourself with the various parts.

Step 2: Fix the Needle Securely in Place

Many sewing machines are sold with the needle secured in place, but if yours doesn't or your needle snaps, begin by twisting the hand dial until the needle lever reaches its highest position. Underneath the arm of your machine, there will be a hole where you fix the needle.

Since needles for sewing machines feature a flat side, ensure that you insert it facing the back of the device. Secure the needle by twisting the needle pin, then try bringing the hand dial towards yourself. You should observe the needle coming down then going back up again. If the needle doesn't fall out when you do this, you'll know that it is fastened appropriately.

Step 3: Wind the Bobbin and Insert It

A sewing machine has 2 sources of thread, a lower thread, and a top thread, all of which are housed in a bobbin. Wind your bobbin by placing a spool of bobbin over the bobbin winder on the upper side. Grab the spool thread, twist it across the guide, and then go to the bobbin. Turn on your bobbin winder and wait until the bobbin gets full, then stops automatically.

Once your bobbin is done winding, insert it into the bobbin cage underneath the needle on the bottom half of your machine. Sometimes the bobbin case is housed inside the machine.

Step 4: Threading a Sewing Machine

You can find the spool of thread over the top of your machine; however, it needs to be unwound and joined to the needle. This is done by grabbing the thread and yanking it up across the thread guide on top, then down around the take-up lever.

Your sewing machine should have small arrows and numbers printed on it to show how to thread your machine. The thread usually follows the following standard pattern: spool pin first, then tension, take-up lever, and finally through the needle, following the thread guides found around those parts. You can thread the needle from the right, the left, or front to back.

Some machines come with an already threaded needle which gives you a hint of the direction, but if yours doesn't, find the final thread guide before your needle – it will be positioned around where you need to thread your needle.

Step 5: Bring Both Threads Outside

With your left hand, pull the needle thread tight towards you. Using your right hand, turn the wheel to form a full needle down/up rotation. Yank the needle thread on your left hand upwards; when you lead your threaded needle upwards, the bobbin thread gets caught and forms a loop over the needle thread.

Bring the tip of your bobbin thread upwards after tugging on one side of the newly formed loop. Alternatively, you can simply let go of the needle thread, slip some scissors between the plate, and presser foot to yank out the bobbin thread that is looped. Now you should be having 2 thread ends, one sticking out from the bobbin and the other from your needle.

Step 6: Plug In Your Sewing Machine and Switch It On

Most machines feature an in-built light that lets you know when the machine is powered up. If your sewing machine includes a power switch, it's usually found at the back or on the right side.

Some devices without a separate switch only need you to plug them in to turn them on. Plug in the pedal as well by placing it in a comfortable position on the machine below your feet.

How To Sew with your Sewing Machine

To sew, follow the following steps:

Step 1: Position the Fabric for Sewing

Twist the hand wheel to lift the needle, then use the presser foot lever to bring the presser foot up. Slip your fabric underneath the needle where you'd like to begin sewing.

The plate usually includes an indicator guide for measuring seam allowances in most machines. Line the edge of your fabric with this guide to help maintain an equal distance from the edge while you sew.

Secure your fabric in position by lowering the presser foot, then lower the needle through your fabric by twisting the handwheel towards yourself.

You can now begin sewing!

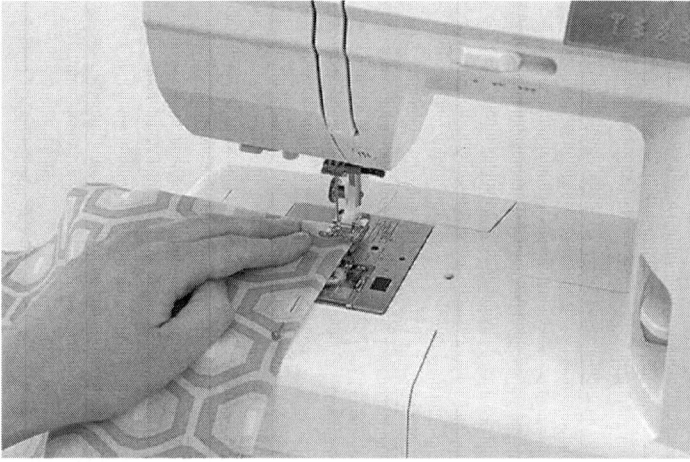

Step 2: Start Sewing

Start sewing by pressing the pedal foot. Feed your fabric below the presser foot while controlling your sewing speed using the foot pedal. If you must add a bit more tension to support your fabric, slide it through the presser foot once more.

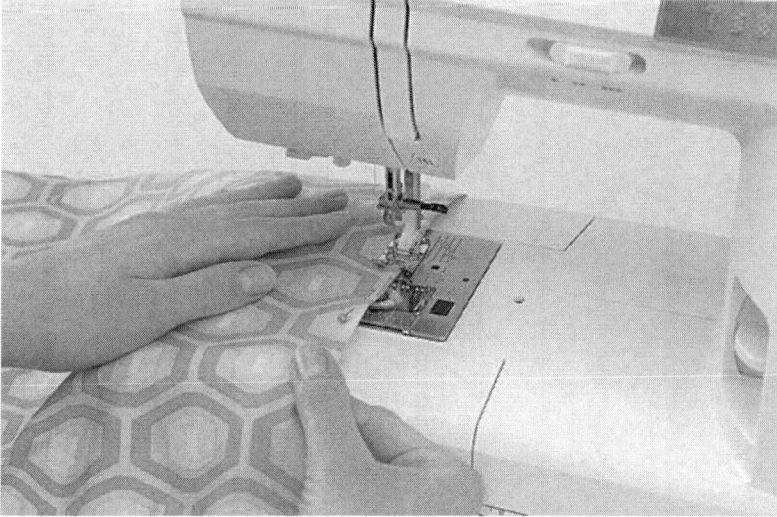

Step 3: Learn to Sew a Sharp Corner

You can turn a corner very easily, even without exhausting the thread. Lower your needle down through the fabric using the handwheel. Lift the presser foot.

Spin your fabric to another position with the needle still in the fabric. Lastly, bring down the presser foot on the newly positioned fabric and continue sewing.

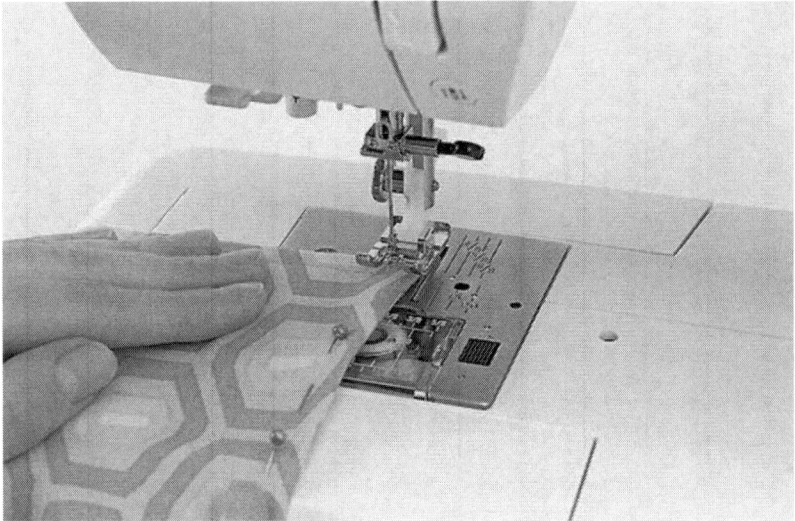

Step 4: Finishing the Stitching Line

Once you are done making a stitching line, make a couple of stitches backward and forward over the line to finish it securely. To stitch towards the back, push the reverse stitch lever and then stitch frontwards by releasing the lever.

Raise the needle, lift the presser foot, then pull the fabric out carefully as it will still be attached to the threads.

Clip off the threads.

Step 5: How to Practice Sewing a Seam

Pin together 2 fabric pieces almost by the edge with the right sides facing each other. The seam should be around 1.3cm (1/2 inch) - 1.5cm (5/8 inch) from the edge. You may sew a single fabric layer to prevent your edges from fraying; however, since the purpose of almost every sewing machine is to attach 2 fabric pieces to each other, then you will have to get comfortable with sewing multiple layers and using several pins.

To add a seam allowance, pin the fabric with the right sides facing each other. This way, the seam allowance will be secured inside the fabric. The side of your fabric that you'd like to be on the outer side once you finish the design is called the "right" side. For fabric that is printed, it is typically the side where the colors seem brighter. On the other hand, the right side for solids may not be that obvious.

Position your pins to be perpendicular to the line where you'll put the seam. You may stitch right over straight pins and take them out later without causing any damage to the fabric, machine, or the pins themselves.

Since you are just getting started, though, it's safer to take the pins out right before you get to them while sewing because accidentally striking a pin can dull your needle or even break it. Make sure to pass up on stitching over the pinheads.

Step 6: Switching to Another Section of the Fabric

When you reach the end of a seam, lift the needle using the handwheel, then take the fabric off the machine. When the needle moves up, you can switch to another section on the fabric. If the needle hasn't reached up to the place where it is housed ("top of its travel" in sewing terms), the fabric can get stuck in the thread when you yank on the ends.

Your sewing machine should include lines indicating the seam allowance – the standard space between the stitching line and the fabric's edge. The line should generally be used at 1.3cm (1/2 inch) or 1.5cm (5/8 inch). You can measure on both sides of the needle using a ruler.

Now that we have gone through the basics of sewing with a sewing machine, how about trying out some fun beginner-friendly sewing projects to take your new machine for a spin!

Chapter 6: Easy Sewing Patterns for Different Types of Clothes

DIY Wool Blanket Coat

Materials and Supplies

- Thread

- Sewing machine

- Pins

- Small plate

- Sharp scissors

- Chalk

- Measuring tape

- Blanket

Directions

Step 1: Grab a blanket and fold it in half to have the shorter ends lined up. Ensure that all sides are aligned.

Step 2: Locate the midpoint of the blanket and mark it. Take an ordinary flat plate and position it over the middle of the top fold so that only half of it lies over the blanket. Cut the piece on top up the middle till you get to the base of your plate, then form a half-circle on the blanket by cutting around the plate.

Step 3: Remove the plate, then cut off the half-circle along the fold.

Step 4: Set your sewing machine to use the zigzag stitch

Step 5: Sew all across the blanket's fresh raw edges using the zigzag stitch.

Step 6: Fold the stitched edges towards the wrong side, then secure in place with pins.

Step 7: Depending on your sewing machine, select a decorative stitch. You can simply use a zig-zag or straight stitch if you don't have a machine with some decorative stitches.

Step 8: Use your preferred stitch to sew along the folded edge.

DIY Beach Dress

Materials and Supplies

- 1 matching thread

- 1 package of bias tape

- 1 yard lightweight woven fabric (this pattern used a lightweight polyester; however, you can also use a lightweight linen blend, lightweight rayon, or chiffon)

Directions

Step 1: Cut out the pieces. Use one of your sleeveless dresses or tank top as a pattern, however, make sure that the neckline is twice as wide to leave enough space for pleating.

Make 2 pieces, one for the back and one for the front of the dress. Ensure that the front neckline is a bit lower than the back one.

Step 2: Find the mid-point of the neckline, then fold the pleats inwards to have them spaced evenly and aligned. Make 6 pleats on the front side and 4 more larger pleats on the backside.

Step 3: Pin the pleats in place, then secure them by sewing a basting stitch across them.

Step 4: Stitch up your shoulder seams.

Step 5: Cut out a length of bias tape enough to go around the whole armhole. With the right sides facing each other, pin the bias tape to the armhole, then secure using a straight seam. Rework the same process for the other sleeve.

Step 6: Next, you'll be dealing with the neckline. Cut out a length of bias tape enough to go across the whole neckline, then stitch it together to create a loop.

With the right sides facing each other, pin the tape to the neckline and use the straight stitch to sew across the whole neckline. If your basting seam is visible, pull it out using a seam ripper.

Step 7: Tuck in the entire bias tape, press then pin in position. Secure the bias tape by sewing across the neck hole and armholes.

Step 8: With the right sides facing each other, sew the side seams up.

Step 9: Hem your dress to your preferred length.

Pom Pom Trim Beach Cover Up

Materials and Supplies

- Pink thread + teal thread

- 6.5 yards of pom pom trim

- Trim for the neckline

- 2 yards of lightweight fabric (This pattern used rayon)

Directions

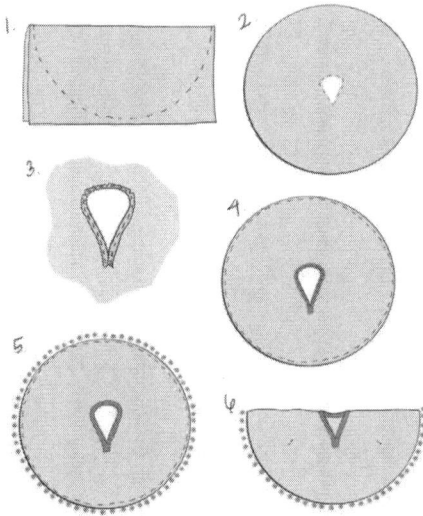

Step 1: Fold your fabric into halves, then carve out a half circle as per figure 1 above. Open the fabric up to reveal a perfect circle.

Step 2: Find the midpoint of your fabric, then cut out a space for your head as desired. This pattern cuts a V-neck on the front side.

Step 3: Fold over your neck-hole's edges two times before hemming in place using the matching thread. To keep the hem flat, cut notches down the curves.

Step 4: Measure the opening of the neck hole, then cut out part of the neckline trim to your desired size. Pin the neckline together, then secure in place by sewing using your matching thread. Use the matching thread to hem the whole circumference of your coverup.

Step 5: When you are through with hemming, pin the pom pom trim along the circumference of your beach coverup, then once again use the matching thread to sew it securely in position.

Step 6: Lastly, fold your coverup into halves, then create 2 little stitches below the armpit on both sides. The small stitches prevent the cloth from slipping around when you put it on and also prevent the sides from being entirely open.

Step 7: Press each of your seams.

Tulip Wrap Skirt Tutorial

Materials and Supplies

- Pins

- Sewing machine

- Scissors

- Matching thread

- 1.5 yards of flowy fabric (knit, rayon or polyester)

Directions

Step 1: Choose one of the shapes illustrated below to cut out the fabric piece, ensuring to make the length of your waist x 2 plus 12 inches-16 inches for the cross-over design on the front side.

The shape above is flatter on the front and is less flowy

*The shape above, on the other hand, is flowier and more curved. This pattern used this. Start by cutting a wide and thick shape of a "V," then round out the sharp edges.

Step 1: Once you have cut the shape out, what follows is hemming your edges.

Step 2: Collect the upper edge of your skirt.

Step 3: Form the bias tape to be as wide as you like x 2 and 1 more inch for the length. Fold the tape over, then press it with an iron in half and iron/press one side a quarter inch towards the inside.

Step 4: Fold either end over and iron.

Step 5: Pin the part that is not folded to the gathered top, then stitch it together using a straight stitch. Fold over, then press.

Step 6: Fold your waistband over to the back side, then pin in place. Stitch a topstitch on the outside of your skirt along the waistband edge.

The steps explained above are illustrated on the image below for easier understanding of the pattern:

Step 7: To the top front of your skirt, attach 2 buttons at 6 to 9 inches apart based on the extent to which you'd like your

skirt to cross over. Create 2 holes for the buttons on the other side at the same width as the buttons. You can create additional holes for adjusting the size of your waist.

If you want to keep the button holes and buttons hidden, stitch a buttonhole on only one side of your waist right before the fifth step.

DIY Embellished Pocket Tees

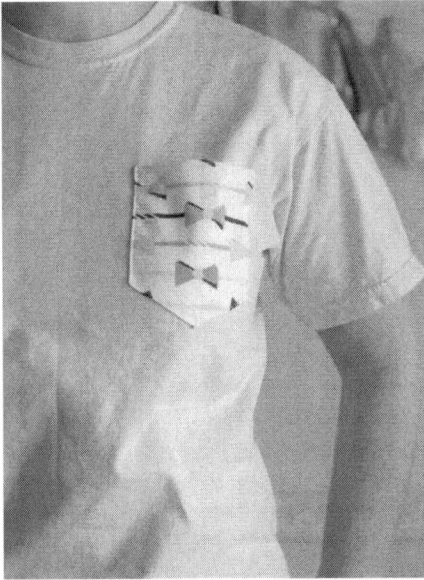

Materials and Supplies

- Pocket Template (download here)[1]

- A scrap of pink horseshoe print, bowtie print, and a piece of Derby Style Fabric

- Matching thread and scissors

- Sewing machine

---

[1] https://www.polkadotchair.com/templates/

- A t-shirt you have washed and dried (this pattern used Comfort Color tees)

- A printout of your favorite State printed on the background like a mirror image

- Heat N Bond Lite

Directions

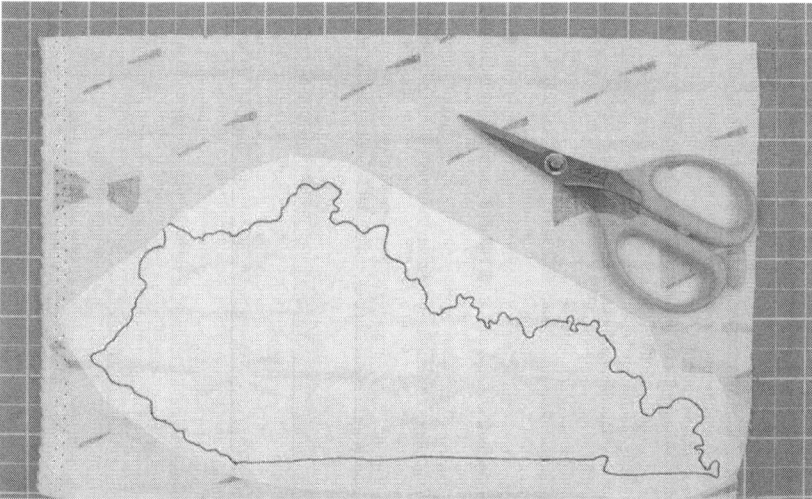

Step 1: On the paper section of your Heat N Bond Lite, trace the state's outline. Cut the shape loosely, then press it onto the Derby Style Bow tie fabric's wrong side. Cut the shape exactly as it is.

Step 2: On another piece of Heat N Bond lite, sketch a heart on the paper section. Cut out the shape and press it on your pink fabric. Trim off the heart.

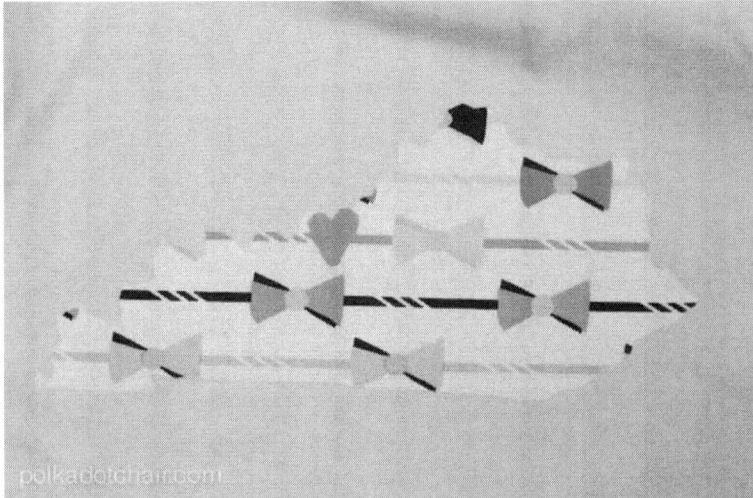

Step 3: Remove the paper backing from the shapes, then iron it in your preferred position on the backside of your t-shirt. Ensure that your shapes are straight. If necessary, you can even use fabric ink to draw a line for guiding you.

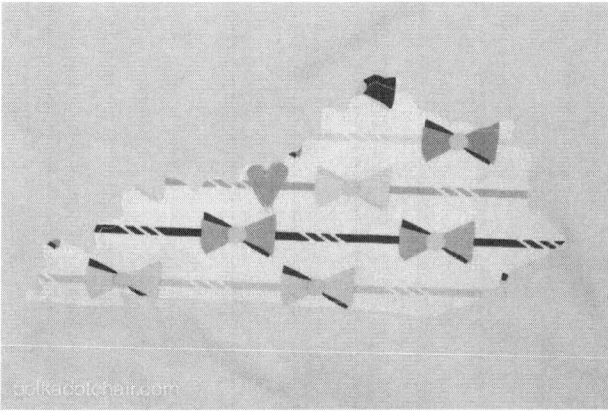

Step 4: Use a simple straight stitch to sew across the silhouette of the shape of the state and the heart.

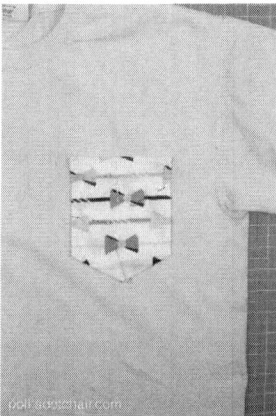

Step 5: Use the bow tie print fabric to cut out 2 pieces for the pocket. Pin and stitch together the 2 pocket pieces, then sew onto the t-shirt.

Chapter 7: Easy Sewing Patterns for Different Types Of Bags

Indestructible Quick Sew Bag

Materials and Supplies

- Hammer

- 1 yard of shoelace, cord, or drawstring

- Setting tool and at least 6 extra-large grommets

- ½ yard of waterproof Oxford fabric

- Yard stick, rotary shears/cutter, small clips, pins, compass or plate

- Double cord stop

Optional: pinking shears, walking foot

Directions

*The completed size of the project in this pattern was 12 inches long and 8 ½ inches wide; however, you can make yours as smaller or bigger as desired.

Step 1: Begin by cutting out a rectangle of 14 ¼ inches in length by 30 inches in width and a circle with a diameter of 9 inches from the waterproof oxford fabric.

Tip: To create a perfect circle, try tracing with a plate.

Step 2: Fold your rectangle widthwise in half, then sew along the side, leaving a seam allowance of ½ inch. This step is completely optional, but it keeps the raw edges from showing on the inside.

Since the fabric is now formed into a tube, take care not to sew through both sides.

Step 3: Pin the circular piece and the base opening in place with the right sides together.

Note: for waterproof oxford, the pinholes are permanent, so ensure that you stick the pins near the raw edges; when you do that, the pinholes will be hidden in the seam allowance.

Slowly sew your fabric together, leaving a seam allowance of ¼ inch. It is not necessary to have a walking foot; however, it makes it simpler to hold the layers in place with no shifting while sewing.

Step 4: Fold the upper raw edge 2 inches towards the inside. If you don't like working with pins, try using little clips to keep the fold in position as you sew. To make the raw edge on the inner side more appealing, first, use the pinking shears to trim it, then sew all across 1 ½ inches from the fold.

Step 5: What follows is installing the grommets. Get the extra-large ones that are suitable for your preferred selection of cords and drawstrings and thicknesses.

All you will require is a hammer and a cheap grommet install kit. Form markings for every grommet first. This pattern used only 6 grommets that were spaced at approximately ¾ inches down from the top and 4 ½ inches apart.

To form the required holes, use the thread scissors to curve a little plus sign. Make the hole a bit wider, enough to push the grommet's male side through – ensure that part is faced within the bin.

Step 6: Position the bottom piece below, then place the other half of the grommet over it. Add the setting tool on top before you begin to hammer.

Step 7: Slip your drawstring through the holes, then cut it at your preferred length. This pattern used a pretty flower shoelace that matched the fabric colors and prints perfectly.

Step 8: Yank the ends of your string through the cord stop.

You are all done!

*You can add stuffed animals, school supplies, clothes, and any other item that requires to be contained.

DIY Grocery Sack Holder

Materials and Supplies

- Fabric Scissors

- ¼ inch wide elastic, 8-10 inches in length

- Coordinating Thread

- Cotton Fabric (optional to have contrasting prints)

- Sewing Machine

Directions

Step 1: Cut your fabric to size. For this pattern, the main striped fabric was cut into a rectangle of 18 by 20 inches, the strap 2 by 10 inches, and the accent piece 5 by 18 inches. You can adjust the measurements very easily according to the fabric you have on hand or to suit your needs.

Below are the pattern pieces:

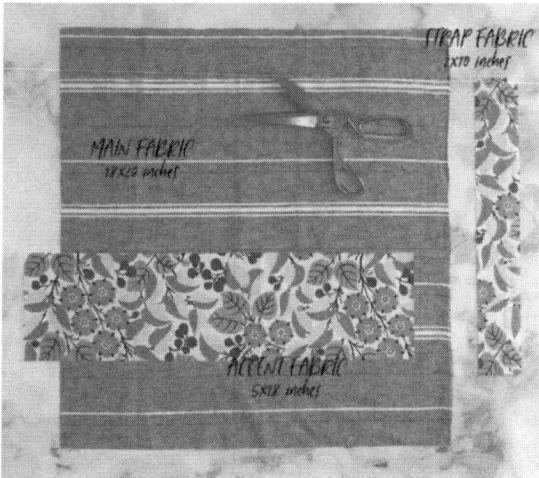

Step 2: With the right sides facing each other, fold the fabric for the strap then stitch across the open edge. Turn the material to have the right side on the outside, then iron the strap to make it crisp.

Step 3: Stitch the accent fabric onto the base end of your main fabric with the right sides facing each other. If desired, add a trim, then press your seam flat.

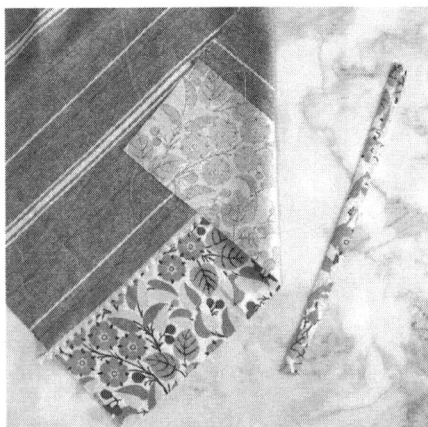

Step 4: Fold your fabric lengthwise to have the right sides together, then stitch across the open edge; the fabric creates a long tube.

Step 5: Slip your strap into the tube, then align the ends with the upper fabric edge. Tuck the straps in position, then align either side of the top edge (concealing the strap fabric inside) then close up the opening by sewing across the top edge.

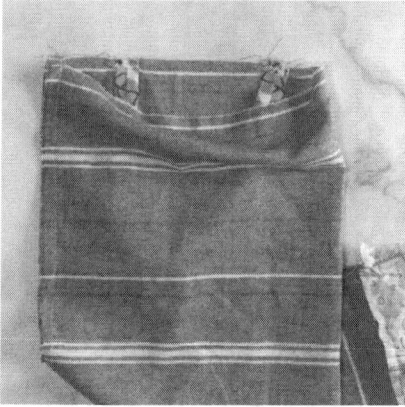

Step 6: Fold over the base edge, then fold it once more to create a covering for the elastic. Stitch down the seam making sure to leave an opening of 2 to 3 inches.

Step 7: Join the end of your elastic to a safety pin, then thread the elastic through the covering you made in the previous step using the safety pin. Take off the safety pin

once you have yanked the elastic all the way through. Stitch together the tips of your elastic. Hide the elastic by sewing the opening of the casing shut.

Step 8: Flip your design to be right side outwards. Insert your grocery bags through the bottom hole of the holder, then when you need one, simply pull them out. The elastic holds the sacks inside with no need for another closure.

Drawstring Bag for Kids

Materials and Supplies

Terry cloth fabric

Cording or drawstring

Heat 'n' Bond and some pieces of coordinating fabrics if you'll include a face

Sewing machine

Directions

Step 1: Cut out the pieces of fabric for your bag. For this pattern, the pieces measured 18 inches in length by 14. (If you'd like the bag to have a face, now is the time to sew it on.)

Step 2: Put the fabrics together with the right sides facing each other, then sew along the bottom edge and both sides; don't forget to leave the seam allowance.

Step 3: Fold the top edge at around 1 inch inwards, then hem it in place as shown below:

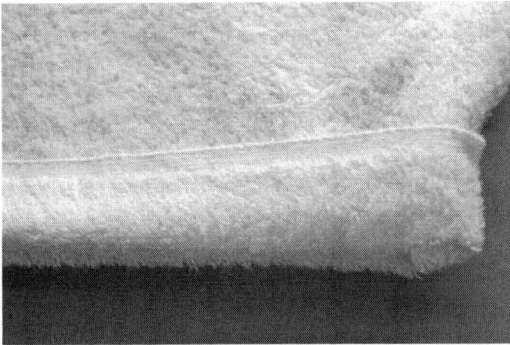

Step 4: Turn your bag to have the right side outward-facing. Form little holes by slitting the side seams you had hemmed earlier.

Step 5: Keep the holes from unfastening by stitching right above them – the hem seam will be underneath the holes.

Step 6: Form 2 more tiny holes on the corners at the bottom of your bag, ensuring that they run through either fabric layers - it's just like making fairly larger buttonholes.

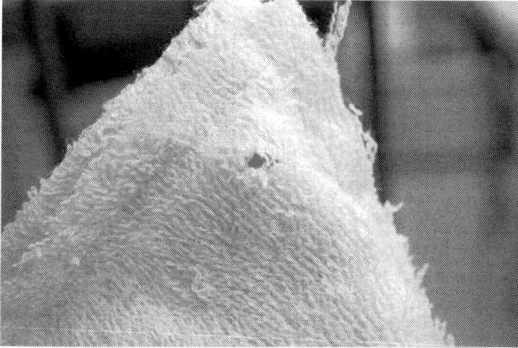

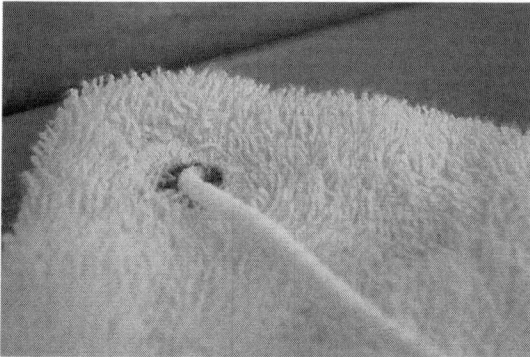

Step 7: Fix a big safety pin to the end of your safety pin, then thread it through to the other side. Pull to have either end of the drawstring at the base of your bag.

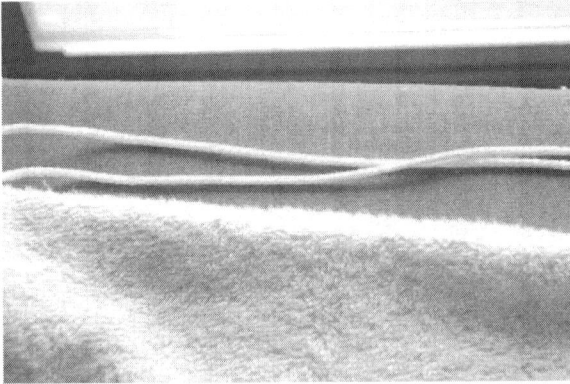

Step 8: Lead one of the drawstrings into the buttonhole, then fasten it to the other string as shown below:

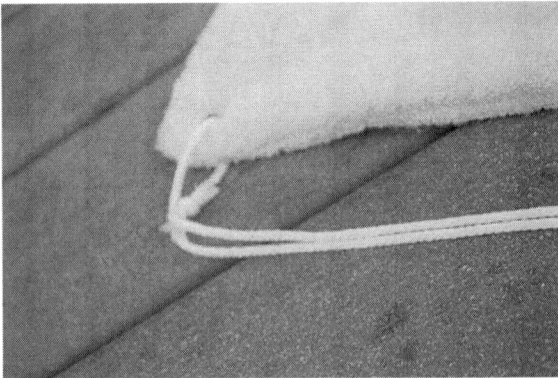

Step 9: Finish by repeating the same process on the remaining side of your bag.

DIY Envelop Laptop Case

Materials and Supplies

- 4 clips

- Pins

- Belt

- Punch pliers

- Fabric

- Iron

- Scissors

- Felt

- Sewing machine (if you'll be using a leather belt, ensure your machine has a leather needle)

- Pencil or tailor's chalk

- Sewing thread in matching color

- Template

Directions

Making a personalized template for your laptop

You will need enough paper (newspaper works just fine), approximately thrice your laptop's size, and a measuring tape. Measure the depth, height, and width of your laptop or you can make it easy by checking online) then sketch the template as explained below:

Note: height + width + ½ inch/1cm (0.5 cm / 1/4″ seam allowance of ¼ inch/1/2cm on both sides). For a wider seam allowance, use 5/8 inch/1 ½ cm.

Step 1: Cut the designs out along the yellow lines to create the template. Put the template towards the left of your felt, then pin in place. Cut the felt along the pattern edge.

Step 2: Place the template over your fabric's left side, then cut it out, leaving a seam allowance of half an inch (1cm) all across the design. To make it easier to cut the precise shape, use a tailor's chalk or pencil to indicate the cutting line leaving a distance of half an inch to your template.

Step 3: Cut out tiny triangles along the edges. Ensure that your triangles are within the seam allowance.

Step 4: Fold the allowance inwards to have the wrong sides facing each other, then press. Make your edges as round and smooth as you can – the small triangles around the edges will help with this.

Step 5: With the wrong sides together, pin your fabric to the felt, then stitch together each side using a straight stitch; the seam you form will be noticeable.

Step 6: Fit your laptop into the case and secure the sides using clips. Grab the belt, wrap it across the center, and then note where to trim it off. Fitting the belt with your laptop inside the uncompleted case is very crucial unless you want to wind up with a length that is too short for your design. Ensure to note down the location of the belt over your fabric. Trim off the extra length of the belt.

Step 7: Unwrap the casing, then stitch your belt onto the design. Be careful to use the points you had marked when the laptop was folded into the case.

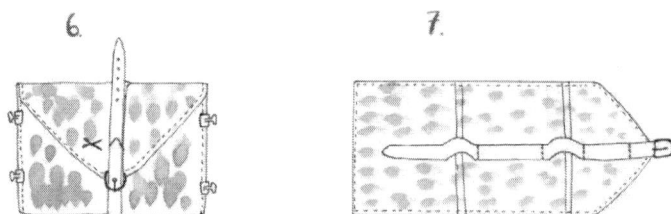

Fig: Step 6 and 7

Step 8: to make the handle, grab the extra belt length you clipped off and stitch it on the upper side. For this pattern, a zigzag stitch worked well. Then, sew both seams on either side. Stitch the handle a couple of times, back and forward, to make it stronger.

When fixing the handle, note down the position with a tailor's chalk or pencil with your laptop inside the envelope case. Ensure you leave enough room between the handle and case where your hand can fit.

Step 9: Pin together the sides of your envelope design, then stitch across the noticeable seam. You can make your seam strong by using a triple straight stitch as we did in this pattern. Be careful that the seam allowance does not get too snug for the laptop.

Step 10: Form 1 or 2 new holes along the belt, and you are done creating a cozy place for your laptop.

Adventure Summer Sling Bag Tutorial

Materials and Supplies

- 2 fat quarters, 1 for exterior, 1 for lining

- ¼ yard accent fabric

- Sewing supplies

Optional: Large button

Directions

Cut out the following pieces from the accent fabric:

- Two pieces of fabric measuring 3 ½ by 8 inches

- 1 strip of fabric with a width of 3 inches and the length trimmed down to 36 inches

Cut out the following measurements from all fat quarters:

- 2 pieces from every fat quarter measuring 8 inches in length by a width of 13 inches

*The fabric pieces are as shown below:

Step 1: To Prepare the Strap for The Sling Bag

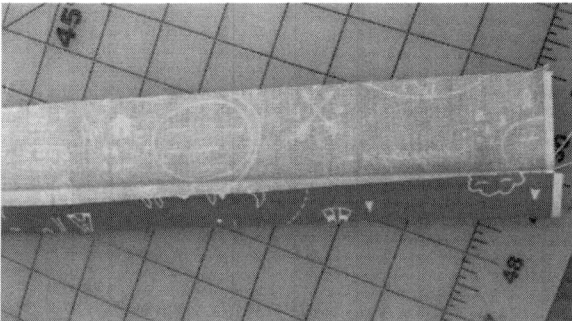

Grab the fabric piece for the strap and fold it lengthwise in half, then press. Unfold the halves, then tuck the length edges within the crease. Cover your raw edges by folding once more along the crease and secure either side of your strap by edge stitching.

For the rest of the design instructions are as follows:

Note: For the seam allowance, make sure to use half an inch unless directed otherwise

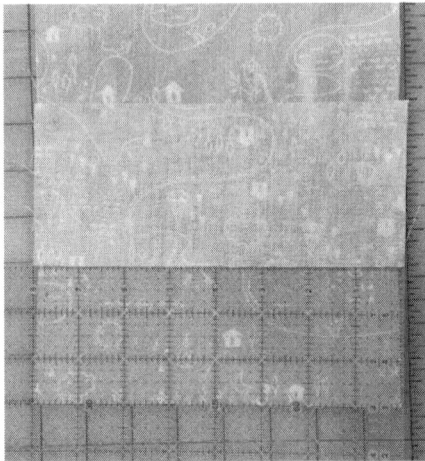

Step 2: With the right side facing upwards, lay out the first outside piece.

Step 3: At 3 inches from the base of the outside piece, lay one of the accent pieces with the wrong side facing upwards.

Step 4: Stitch together the outside and accent pieces, leaving a seam allowance of ¼ inches.

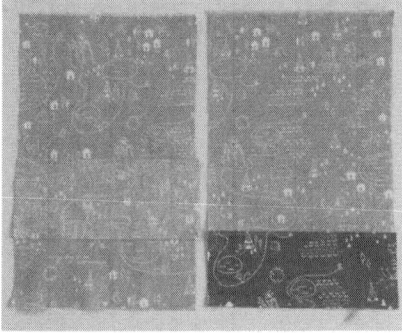

Step 5: Fold the top of your accent piece, then iron before topstitching across the edge. Rework the same process for the other outside piece.

Step 6: At 4 inches from the top of one of the outside pieces, line up both raw edges of your strap as shown above, then pin in place as shown below:

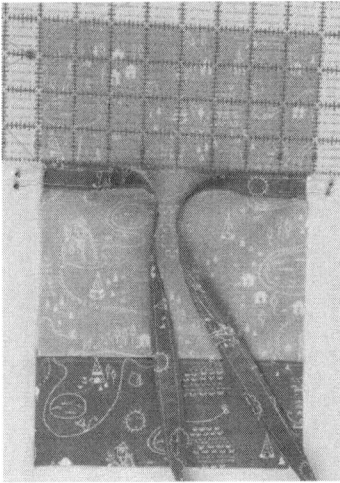

Step 7: Put together both pieces for the outside with the right sides facing each other. Stitch along either side and the base.

Step 8: Put together the 2 pieces for the lining with the right sides facing each other. Stitch along both sides and the base, making sure to leave a space of 3 to 4 inches wide.

Step 9: Trim the corners along the bottom of both the lining and exterior pieces as shown below:

Step 10: Turn the outside piece of your sling bag to have the right-side facing outwards.

Step 11: Insert the outer piece into the inside of the bag's lining. Align your side seams and the upper edge, ensuring that the strap is not in the way as well.

Step 12: Stitch across the upper edge of your bag.

Step 13: Using the spacing at the base of your lining piece, turn your bag to have the right-side facing outwards.

Step 14: Sew the spacing at the base of the lining shut.

Step 15: Stuff the lining inside the bag. Fold across the stitched line, then iron to flatten. sew the opening at the top of your bag

Optional Step: You may stitch a big button on one side of your spacing to aid in keeping it better closed.

Chapter 8: Easy Outdoor Sewing Projects For Beginners

DIY Fruit Slice Pillows

Materials and Supplies

- Cotton cord for pipping

- Scotch tape

- Sewing machine

- Needle and thread

- Black felt sheet for the seeds of dragon fruit, kiwi, or watermelon

- ½ yard of red felt for the watermelon or yellow, green or orange felt for citrus slices

- ½ yard white felt

- 1 ½ yards of cotton fabric in your preferred color

Directions

Step 1: You will require cutting out the pieces that follow: two 2 by 4 inches strips, two 14-inch circles, and four 22 by 2 inches strips curved on the bias (meaning on a diagonal).

For this, fold the fabric in half, cut out the circles on the upper side, and cut a 44 by 4 inches strip across the fold below. Open the fabric up and cut 4 shorter strips measuring 22 by 2 inches on the bias. You can adjust the sizes according to your needs.

Step 2: Carve out the fruit pieces from their corresponding felt:

Kiwi: 1 six-inch circle, a number of black seeds

Dragon fruit: 1 ten-inch white circle with an edge that is wavy, several black seeds

Watermelon: 1 nine-inch red circle, 1 ten-inch white circle, several black seeds

Citrus slices: 8 wedges from your preferred color and 1 ten-inch white circle

Step 3: Use the sewing machine to sew together the felt pieces, then sew the felt pieces to one of the fabric circles. This forms the front piece. Stitch across the edges of the pieces of felt using your foot's edge as a guide to make even stitches, or you can sew near the edge if you are more comfortable with that or are more experienced.

Make the stitches as directed below:

Kiwi: Sew the white felt onto the fabric circle and sew the seeds on the fabric circle around the white felt.

Dragon fruit: Attach the seeds onto the white felt by sewing, then stitch the felt to the circle of fabric.

Watermelon: Stitch your seeds onto the red felt, sew the red felt onto the white felt, and secure the white felt to the fabric circle with stitches.

Citrus slices: Sew your wedges onto the white circle, then sew the white circle over the fabric circle.

Step 4: Prepare the side piece by sewing together two 22-inch by 4 inches pieces to create one long piece, then put it aside.

Step 5: The next thing to do is form the bias tape. Grab 2 of the pieces you cut on the bias, align them by their corners, and then sew diagonally. Open your seam, flatten by ironing, fold 1" inwards on one of the shorter edges, and then flatten by ironing.

Fold your strip lengthwise in half and iron it to make it easier to work with. Rework the same process with the 2 strips remaining.

Step 6: Slip the cord into the lengthy piping you just made. Make sure it begins at the base of the 1-inch piece you had ironed flat.

Step 7: Pin your piping's raw edges to the edge on the right side of one circle. Baste your trim in position with a zipper foot and stop at approximately 1" from the end. Trim off the extra cord to have both cord ends meeting perfectly.

Secure those raw edges using a piece of scotch tape, then slide them into the end that is folded over. Finish sewing them shut. Rework the same process with the other circles and piping pieces.

Step 8: Stitch the pillow together and complete it. Take the side piece you were stitching before, then pin it over the piping sewed to the front piece. It will not fit perfectly, and that's how it's supposed to be. Leave the extra to hang. Starting at approximately 1" from the short edge, sew along the circle's circumference.

Step 9: Remove the pieces from your sewing machine, then pin together the short edges. This is going to fit perfectly to the side of your circle piece. Leaving half an inch seam, sew an even line along the side edge.

Step 10: With the right side inside, pin together the back piece to the remaining end of your side piece, then stitch firmly in place. Make sure to leave approximately 4" of space not stitched for turning the fabric.

Step 11: Turn the pillow to have the right side outward-facing, then stuff.

Step 12: Use a slip stitch to hand sew together the last couple of stitches left. Rework the same process for all the other fruit slice pillows.

15-Minute DIY Picnic Blanket

Materials and Supplies

- 1 cotton tablecloth – we used 48 by 60 inches for this pattern

- 3 yards twill ribbon

- 1 waterproof or vinyl tablecloth – equal size to the cotton tablecloth

- Matching thread of the tablecloths

Directions

Step 1: Cut the twill ribbon into 2 equal pieces. Each piece will be 1 ½ yards in length. Fold both pieces into halves.

Step 2: With the wrong side facing outwards, lay out your vinyl tablecloth. Place the cotton tablecloth over the vinyl one with the right side facing upwards, ensuring that every edge is aligned.

On one of the shorter sides of your tablecloths, measure 24 inches from both ends, then tuck the twill ribbon's folded side between the 2 tablecloths as shown below:

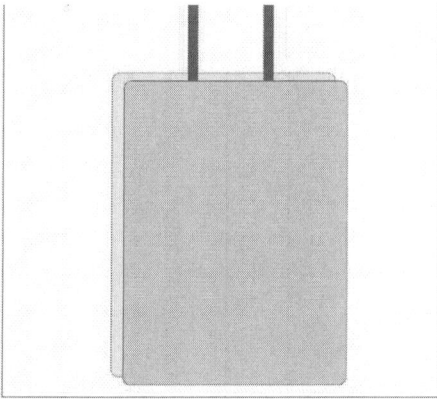

Step 3: Pin together both tablecloths firmly in place to prevent shifting while sewing.

Step 4: Stitch along each of the 4 sides of your cloths and backstitch around the 2 sections the twill ribbon crosses. It's that easy!

Tip: To fold the picnic blanket, fold it lengthwise in half, then roll it up from below in the same way as a sleeping bag.

Outdoor Chaise Slip Covers

Materials and Supplies

- Large bath sheets or beach towels (or terry cloth fabric) -we needed 2 ½ towels for each chaise

- Pencil

- Scissors

- Sewing machine

- Matching thread

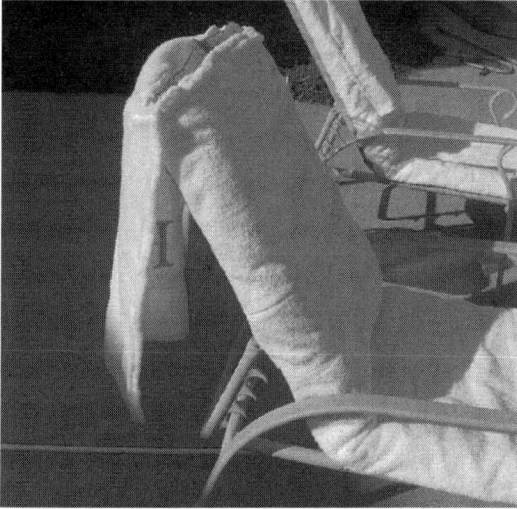

As illustrated in the image above, this pattern is comprised of 3 pieces – a flap, the underside, and the top. It can basically be described as an elongated pillowcase that includes a flap.

Directions

Step 1: Clean your towels using hot water to do away with the extra lint and for shrinkage.

Step 2: Begin to make the patter by placing the cushion of your chaise over one towel.

Step 3: You can pass this step if the length of your towel is enough. If you have shorter towels, use the excess piece of your towel cut from the long side to fill up the space left. Ensure to position your seam at the opening on the top side of your slipcover so that the flap will hide it.

Step 4: Once you have achieved the right length for the top piece, cut the second towel in the same way for the bottom piece.

Step 5: When you finish cutting out both pieces with equal length, pin them together in place having the right sides facing each other. Stitch along the bottom and the 2 sides. As shown in the image below, your design now resembles a sleeping bag:

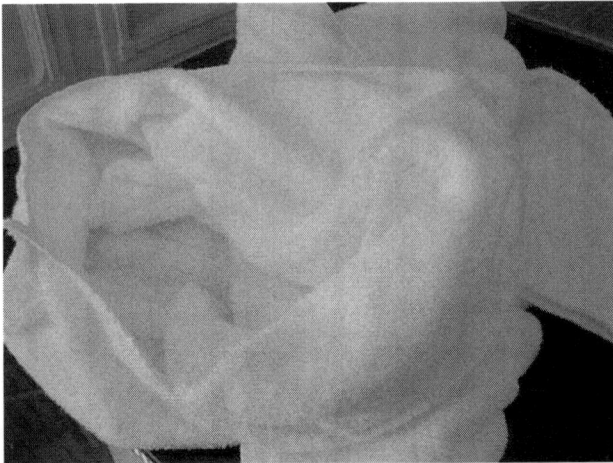

Step 6: Turn your work to have the right-side facing outwards.

Step 7: Smoothen and straighten the corners of your slipcover - if need be, press them.

Adding the Slipcover Flap

For the flap, cut your third towel widthwise in half.

Measure your chaise, then cut the towel to fit the edge at the backside of your slipcover. If you cut the towel to fit, make sure to hem all sides of your flap piece. (Don't worry, as the flap will cover the seams you make.)

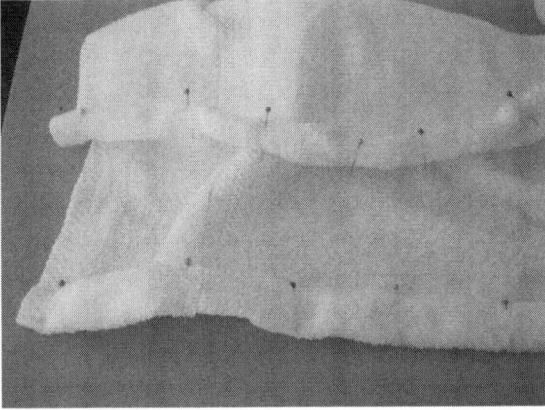

With the right sides together, sew your flap to the backside of your slipcover. Flip the flap over the cushion to test it out.

*When the towel slipcovers become dirty, you can just take them off and clean them.

Gardening Knee Pad Tutorial

Materials and Supplies

- 1 kickboard

- ½ yard of oilcloth

- 12-inch Pleather

- Kam snaps

Directions

Step 1: Split your kickboard into half; you can use both halves to make 2 gardening pads, or just make one and do away with the other half of the kickboard.

Step 2: Make a pillowcase for your kickboard half, leaving a seam allowance of 1 inch on each side. Leave a 4-inch allowance on the upper edge for adding the handles and snaps.

Step 3: Sew along either side and the bottom leaving a seam allowance of 3/8 inches. Snip off the corners, then turn your design to have the right-side facing outwards.

Step 4: Insert the kickboard into the case to ensure it fits. If necessary, stitch your sides smaller. Fold the upper edge inwards, then clip or pin in place. Finish the upper edge by sewing it down.

Step 5: Cut out 2 handles from the pleather. For this pattern, we cut out 2 strips 1.5 inches wide with rounded ends as shown in the image below, then fold lengthwise in half and stitch across the edge:

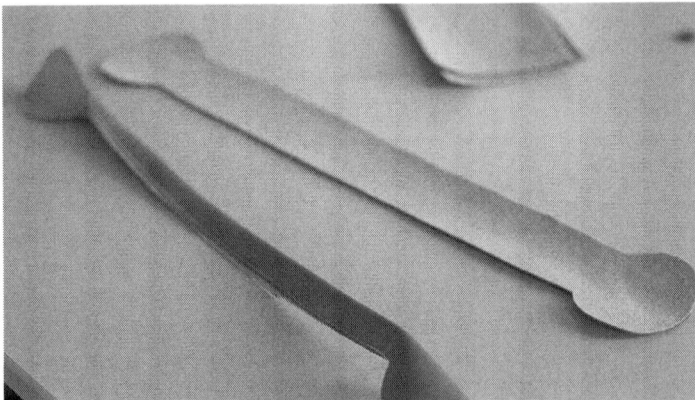

Step 6: Pin the rounded ends of the handles at 2 inches below the upper edge of your gardening mat. Make sure to turn your fabric wrong side outwards to sew the handles on.

The image below shows how it will look like once done sewing the handles from inside out:

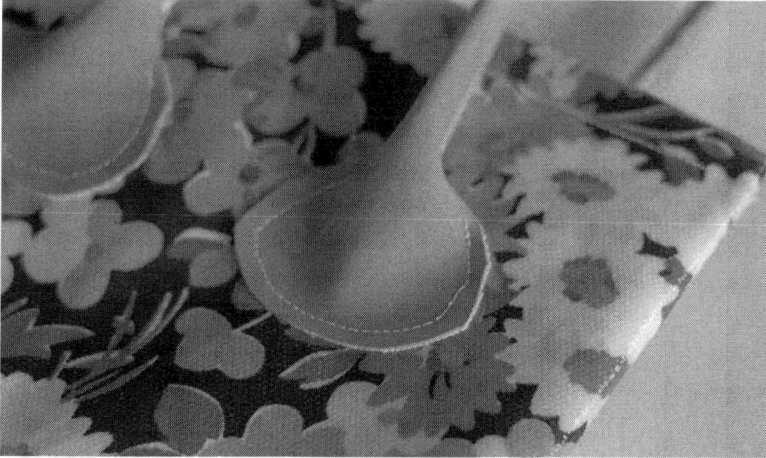

Step 7: For closure on the end of the open knee pad, use snaps or Velcro. This pattern added 2 snaps to keep foam inside:

*Your gardening knee pads are ready for use!

DIY Pouf Ottoman Table/Seat for The Patio

Materials and Supplies

- Rotary cutter

- Foam

- Scissors and pins

- Batting

- Large zipper

- Cutting mat

- Straight edge ruler

- 1 ½ yards of home decor upholstery fabric

Directions

Step 1: Cut Out the Fabric

To begin, measure then cut the fabric. Cut out 6 squares that are evenly sized for a cube. This pattern used squares measuring 18 by 18 inches which yields a pouf measuring approximately 16 inches wide and high after leaving the seam allowance.

Step 2: Adding the Zipper

We'll first sew in the zipper where you unzip it first, then pin either side to one square each.

Step 3: Proceed to Sew

With your zipper open, pin it in place then zip it back up once done.

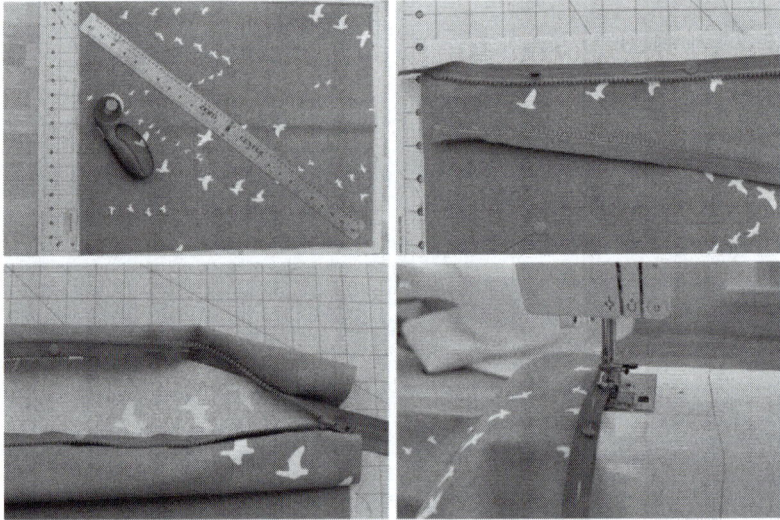

Step 4: Sew On 2 More Squares

Add 2 more squares to the 2 that are joined by the zipper to form one huge row of 4 connected squares. To do this, lay one square with the right side facing up over the square to the furthest right, which has the wrong side facing downwards.

Pin in place along the edge, then sew. Rework the same process until you have joined each of the 4 squares in a single row and all seams are on the inner side of the fabric (when you look at the row with the right side facing upwards, you should not see any seam).

Form a square tunnel that is inside out by connecting both ends of the row. Stitch across the seam formed when both pieces meet. The image below shows an illustration of how the pouf will come together:

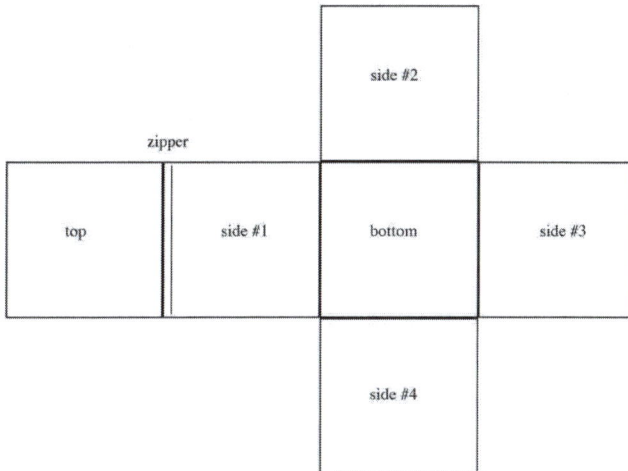

side #2

zipper

| top | side #1 | bottom | side #3 |

side #4

*Since all sides will touch eventually, don't worry if you find yourself out of order so long as once you are done sewing in the seams, you have a way of turning your design to be right side outwards.

Step 5: Adding Another Square to The Square Tunnel

With the wrong side facing upwards (to keep the seams hidden inside the cube), sew on another square onto the square tunnel.

Step 6: Stitch With Your Zipper Opened

Complete the cube by repeating step 5 with the right side of your fabric inside and the zipper open. We keep the zipper open so that once you are done stitching on the last square, you can simply turn the fabric right side outwards.

Step 7: Filling

Fill the pouf with batting and foam, then zip it shut, and you are done!

It works just fine as a table or seat in the patio.

Conclusion

As you have seen, using a sewing machine is very easy; there's really nothing to it. Once you have familiarized yourself with the various parts of a sewing machine, all you need to do is practice and practice, and in no time, you will start to create your own amazing designs.

Don't worry if they come out a little crooked at the beginning. The more you keep sewing, the more perfect they will become.

Printed in Great Britain
by Amazon

16530318R00070